Table of Contents

Introduction 5

Chapter 1: Understanding Digital Marketing Fundamentals 8

    1.1 What is Digital Marketing? 8

    1.2 Importance of Digital Marketing in Today's World 9

    1.3 Key Concepts in Digital Marketing 11

    1.4 Digital Marketing Strategies Overview 12

    1.5 Setting Realistic Goals and KPIs 14

    1.6 Understanding the Buyer's Journey in Digital Marketing 16

Chapter 2: Building Your Online Presence 19

    2.1 Creating a Website That Converts 19

    2.2 Search Engine Optimization (SEO) Basics 22

    2.3 Leveraging Content Marketing 24

    2.4 Social Media Marketing Essentials 26

    2.5 Email Marketing Strategies 28

    2.6 Online Reputation Management 30

Chapter 3: Understanding Digital Advertising 33

    3.1 Introduction to Digital Advertising 33

    3.2 Google Ads Fundamentals 35

3.3 Social Media Advertising Platforms 36

3.4 Display Advertising Strategies.............................. 38

3.5 Video Advertising 39

3.6 Measuring Advertising Performance 41

Chapter 4: Engaging with Your Audience 44

4.1 Building a Community Around Your Brand 44

4.2 Content Personalization and Customization....... 45

4.3 Influencer Marketing Strategies 46

4.4 Interactive Content Strategies 47

4.5 Customer Relationship Management (CRM) 49

4.6 Harnessing the Power of User-Generated Content 50

5.1 Introduction to Digital Analytics 52

5.2 Website Analytics Basics 55

5.3 Social Media Analytics 57

5.4 Email Campaign Analytics 60

5.5 Advertising Analytics.. 63

5.6 Data-Driven Decision Making............................... 65

6.1 Mobile Marketing Strategies 68

6.2 Location-Based Marketing 71

6.3 Mobile Advertising Platforms 74

6.4 Optimizing for Voice Search................................. 76

6.5 Mobile App Marketing 79

6.6 Measuring Mobile and Local Marketing Effectiveness 81

Chapter 7: E-commerce and Online Sales Strategies 85

7.1 Introduction to E-commerce 85

7.2 Creating a Seamless Online Shopping Experience 86

7.3 E-commerce SEO and SEM 88

7.4 Cart Abandonment Recovery Strategies 89

7.5 Personalization in E-commerce 90

7.6 Fulfillment and Customer Service in E-commerce 92

Chapter 8: Emerging Trends in Digital Marketing 95

8.1 Artificial Intelligence (AI) in Marketing 95

8.2 Voice Search and Smart Speakers 97

8.3 Augmented Reality (AR) and Virtual Reality (VR) Marketing 99

8.4 Chatbots and Conversational Marketing 101

8.5 Video Marketing Trends 102

8.6 Privacy and Data Protection in Digital Marketing 104

Chapter 9: Crafting Your Digital Marketing Strategy .. 107

9.1 Assessing Your Current Marketing Situation 107

9.2 Defining Your Target Audience and Value Proposition 109

9.3 Developing a Comprehensive Marketing Plan .. 111

9.4 Implementation and Execution 112

9.5 Monitoring and Measuring Performance 114

9.6 Continuous Learning and Adaptation 115

Conclusion 118

Introduction

Welcome to the dynamic world of digital marketing! In this era of rapid technological advancement and interconnectedness, the landscape of marketing has undergone a profound transformation. Traditional methods have evolved, making way for digital strategies that are not only innovative but also indispensable for businesses of all sizes.

Whether you're a seasoned entrepreneur looking to expand your online presence or a newcomer eager to delve into the realm of digital marketing, this beginner's guide will serve as your compass in navigating the digital marketing terrain of 2024.

In the pages that follow, we'll embark on a journey together, exploring the fundamental principles, latest trends, and best practices that define the contemporary digital marketing ecosystem. From understanding the importance of establishing a strong online presence to mastering the art of crafting compelling content and leveraging the power of social media platforms, this guide will equip you with the knowledge and tools you need to thrive in the digital marketplace.

Moreover, we'll delve into the intricacies of search engine optimization (SEO), pay-per-click (PPC) advertising, email marketing, and other essential components of a comprehensive digital marketing strategy. Through real-world examples, case studies, and actionable insights, you'll gain a deeper understanding of how these tactics work synergistically to drive traffic, generate leads, and foster meaningful engagement with your target audience.

Whether you're aiming to promote a product, raise brand awareness, or drive conversions, the principles of digital marketing remain universal.

By embracing innovation, staying abreast of emerging trends, and adopting a data-driven approach, you'll be well-positioned to thrive in the competitive digital landscape of 2024 and beyond.

So, without further ado, let's embark on this journey together and unlock the boundless opportunities that digital marketing has to offer. Whether you're a novice or a seasoned marketer, there's always something new to learn, and the adventure begins right here.

Chapter 1: Understanding Digital Marketing Fundamentals

1.1 What is Digital Marketing?

Digital marketing encompasses all marketing efforts that utilize electronic devices or the internet. This includes various online channels such as search engines, social media, email, websites, and mobile apps to connect with current and prospective customers. The scope of digital marketing is vast, covering a range of activities from content creation and distribution to data analysis and optimization.

Definition and Scope

At its core, digital marketing aims to promote brands, products, or services through digital channels to reach and engage target audiences. Its scope extends beyond traditional marketing methods by leveraging the power of technology to deliver personalized and targeted messaging. This flexibility allows businesses to adapt their marketing strategies in real-time based on consumer behavior and market trends.

Evolution of Digital Marketing

Digital marketing has evolved significantly over the years, driven by advancements in technology and changes in consumer behavior. Initially, digital marketing mainly focused on email and websites. However, with the rise of social media, mobile devices, and big data analytics, the landscape has transformed dramatically. Today, digital marketing encompasses a diverse array of tactics, including search engine optimization (SEO), content marketing, social media marketing, pay-per-click advertising, and more.

1.2 Importance of Digital Marketing in Today's World

In today's digital age, the significance of digital marketing cannot be overstated. The widespread adoption of digital technologies has fundamentally altered the way businesses interact with their customers and conduct marketing activities.

Impact of Digitalization on Marketing

Digitalization has democratized marketing, providing businesses of all sizes with the opportunity to reach global audiences without the need for significant financial investment. Unlike traditional marketing methods, which often require substantial budgets for advertising space or airtime, digital marketing offers cost-effective alternatives that allow even small businesses to compete on a level playing field.

Advantages of Digital Marketing over Traditional Marketing

One of the key advantages of digital marketing is its ability to target specific demographics with precision. Through data analytics and audience segmentation, marketers can tailor their messages to resonate with the interests and preferences of individual consumers. This level of personalization not only enhances the effectiveness of marketing campaigns but also fosters stronger customer relationships and brand loyalty.

1.3 Key Concepts in Digital Marketing

To navigate the complexities of digital marketing effectively, it is essential to understand some key concepts that underpin the discipline.

Digital Platforms and Channels

Digital marketing operates across a diverse range of platforms and channels, each offering unique opportunities for engagement. These may include search engines like Google, social media platforms such as Facebook and Instagram, email marketing platforms like Mailchimp, and content management systems like WordPress. By leveraging the strengths of each channel, marketers can create integrated campaigns that maximize reach and impact.

Target Audience and Personas

Central to any digital marketing strategy is a clear understanding of the target audience. Marketers must conduct thorough research to identify their ideal customers' demographics, interests, and pain points. Developing detailed buyer personas can help marketers empathize with their audience and tailor content and messaging to address their specific needs and preferences.

1.4 Digital Marketing Strategies Overview

Digital marketing strategies encompass a broad spectrum of tactics designed to achieve specific business objectives.

Introduction to Various Digital Marketing Strategies

Some common digital marketing strategies include:

- **Search Engine Optimization (SEO)**: Optimizing website content to improve visibility and ranking on search engine results pages.

- **Content Marketing**: Creating and distributing valuable, relevant content to attract and engage a target audience.

- **Social Media Marketing**: Leveraging social media platforms to build brand awareness, drive traffic, and foster customer relationships.

- **Email Marketing**: Sending targeted emails to prospects and customers to promote products, share news, and nurture leads.

- **Pay-Per-Click Advertising (PPC)**: Placing ads on search engines or social media platforms and paying only when users click on them.

- **Influencer Marketing**: Partnering with influencers or industry experts to promote products or services to their followers.

Choosing the Right Strategy for Your Business

The most effective digital marketing strategy for a business depends on various factors, including its industry, target audience, budget, and objectives. A comprehensive marketing strategy often combines multiple tactics to create a cohesive and integrated approach. It's essential to continually evaluate and refine strategies based on performance metrics and market dynamics.

1.5 Setting Realistic Goals and KPIs

Setting clear and measurable goals is crucial for the success of any digital marketing campaign.

Defining SMART Goals

SMART goals are Specific, Measurable, Achievable, Relevant, and Time-bound. Examples of SMART goals in digital marketing might include increasing website traffic by 20% within six months, generating 100 new leads per month, or improving conversion rates by 15% year-over-year. By establishing concrete objectives, marketers can track progress and adjust strategies accordingly.

Identifying Key Performance Indicators (KPIs)

Key performance indicators (KPIs) are metrics used to evaluate the performance of marketing initiatives and measure progress toward goals. Common KPIs in digital marketing include website traffic, conversion rates, click-through rates, social media engagement, and return on investment (ROI). By monitoring KPIs regularly, marketers can identify areas for improvement and optimize their campaigns for better results.

1.6 Understanding the Buyer's Journey in Digital Marketing

The buyer's journey refers to the process that consumers go through when making a purchasing decision. In digital marketing, understanding and mapping the buyer's journey is essential for delivering relevant content and guiding prospects toward conversion.

Awareness, Consideration, and Decision Stages

The buyer's journey typically consists of three stages:

1. **Awareness**: The buyer becomes aware of a need or problem and begins researching potential solutions.

2. **Consideration**: The buyer evaluates different options and considers the pros and cons of each.

3. **Decision**: The buyer makes a purchase decision based on their research and evaluation.

Mapping Content to Each Stage

Effective digital marketing involves creating content that addresses the needs and concerns of buyers at each stage of the journey. During the awareness stage, informational content such as blog posts, articles, and infographics can help educate and inspire prospects. In the consideration stage, comparison guides, case studies, and product demos may be more relevant. Finally, during the decision stage, persuasive content like customer testimonials, reviews, and promotional offers can help nudge prospects toward conversion.

By understanding the dynamics of the buyer's journey and aligning marketing efforts accordingly, businesses can effectively engage prospects at every step of the decision-making process and drive meaningful results.

Chapter 2: Building Your Online Presence

In the vast landscape of the digital realm, crafting an effective online presence is akin to constructing a sturdy edifice in a bustling metropolis. Every brick laid, every window polished, contributes to the overall impression visitors receive. It's not merely about existing online; it's about thriving, captivating, and converting. Chapter 2 delves into the intricacies of building this virtual citadel, where each facet, from website design to reputation management, plays a pivotal role in attracting and retaining the attention of your audience.

2.1 Creating a Website That Converts

The digital storefront of any business is its website - a virtual manifestation of its ethos, products, and services. However, mere existence in the digital sphere is insufficient; the website must convert visitors into customers, leads, or loyal followers. Effective website design goes beyond aesthetics; it's about functionality, usability, and intuitiveness.

Website Design Best Practices

1. **Simplicity**: Embrace the elegance of simplicity in design. Cluttered interfaces overwhelm users and deter them from exploring further. Streamlined layouts, intuitive navigation, and clear calls-to-action (CTAs) guide visitors seamlessly through the site.

2. **Responsive Design**: With the proliferation of mobile devices, a responsive website is indispensable. Ensuring compatibility across various screen sizes and resolutions enhances user experience and accessibility, fostering engagement and satisfaction.

3. **Visual Hierarchy**: Employ visual hierarchy to prioritize content and guide user attention. Utilize contrasting colors, varying font sizes, and strategic placement to emphasize essential elements such as headlines, CTAs, and product offerings.

User Experience (UX) Optimization

1. **Load Speed**: In the digital age, patience is a rare virtue. Optimize website load speed to prevent user frustration and high bounce rates. Compress images, minimize HTTP requests, and leverage caching techniques to expedite load times.

2. **Intuitive Navigation**: Simplify navigation to facilitate effortless exploration. Implement clear menus, breadcrumbs, and search functionalities to empower users in finding relevant information swiftly.

3. **Conversion Paths**: Design conversion paths that guide visitors towards desired actions, whether it's making a purchase, signing up for a newsletter, or contacting the company. Eliminate unnecessary steps and friction points to streamline the conversion process.

2.2 Search Engine Optimization (SEO) Basics

In the labyrinthine expanse of the internet, visibility is paramount. Search Engine Optimization (SEO) serves as the compass, guiding users to discover your digital abode amidst the myriad of competitors.

On-Page and Off-Page SEO

1. **On-Page Optimization**: Fine-tune on-page elements such as meta titles, descriptions, headings, and content to align with targeted keywords and improve search engine rankings. Create high-quality, relevant content that

resonates with both users and search algorithms.

2. **Off-Page Optimization**: Cultivate a robust backlink profile through strategic link-building initiatives. Seek opportunities for guest blogging, collaborations, and directory submissions to enhance domain authority and amplify online visibility.

Keyword Research and Implementation

1. **Keyword Research**: Embark on a quest for the Holy Grail of keywords - phrases that encapsulate user intent, relevance, and search volume. Leverage tools like Google Keyword Planner, SEMrush, and Ahrefs to unearth untapped keyword opportunities and refine targeting strategies.

2. **Keyword Implementation**: Seamlessly integrate target keywords into website content, meta tags, URLs, and anchor texts. Strike a harmonious balance between optimization and natural language flow to avoid keyword stuffing and maintain readability.

2.3 Leveraging Content Marketing

Content is the lifeblood of the digital ecosystem - a potent elixir that nourishes, informs, and captivates audiences. From insightful blogs to captivating videos, content marketing encompasses a diverse array of mediums and strategies aimed at resonating with target audiences.

Types of Content

1. **Blogs**: Embark on a literary odyssey with engaging blog posts that entertain, educate, and inspire. Address pain points, provide solutions, and establish thought

leadership within your niche through informative and compelling content.

2. **Videos**: Embrace the power of visual storytelling with immersive video content. From product demonstrations to behind-the-scenes glimpses, videos foster authenticity, trust, and emotional connections with viewers.

3. **Infographics**: Transform data into digestible visual narratives with captivating infographics. Condense complex information into visually appealing graphics that educate and entertain, catering to the short attention spans of modern audiences.

Content Distribution Strategies

1. **Social Media**: Amplify content reach and engagement through strategic social media distribution. Tailor content formats

and messaging to align with platform nuances, leveraging hashtags, captions, and multimedia to captivate audiences across diverse channels.

2. **Email Newsletters**: Cultivate a loyal audience base through curated email newsletters. Deliver value-packed content directly to subscribers' inboxes, nurturing relationships, and fostering brand loyalty through personalized communication.

3. **Syndication and Partnerships**: Forge symbiotic relationships with industry peers and influencers through content syndication and partnerships. Collaborate on guest posts, podcasts, and joint ventures to expand reach and tap into new audience segments.

2.4 Social Media Marketing Essentials

In the bustling digital agora of social media, brands vie for attention amidst the cacophony of tweets, posts, and stories. Crafting a compelling social media presence requires strategic platform selection, engaging content creation, and community cultivation.

Platform Selection and Optimization

1. **Audience Analysis**: Conduct thorough audience research to identify the social media platforms frequented by your target demographics. Tailor platform selection based on user demographics, interests, and engagement preferences.

2. **Profile Optimization**: Optimize social media profiles with captivating visuals, compelling bios, and relevant keywords. Ensure consistency in branding elements across platforms to enhance recognition and reinforce brand identity.

Crafting Engaging Social Media Posts

1. **Visual Content**: Capture attention amidst the scrolling frenzy with visually stunning imagery and graphics. Leverage eye-catching visuals, GIFs, and videos to stop thumbs and ignite curiosity.

2. **Compelling Copy**: Craft concise, compelling copy that resonates with your audience's aspirations, pain points, and interests. Embrace storytelling, humor, and emotion to evoke engagement and foster meaningful connections.

2.5 Email Marketing Strategies

Amidst the deluge of digital noise, email remains a stalwart beacon of direct communication with your audience. From lead generation to nurturing, email marketing strategies encompass a spectrum of tactics aimed at cultivating relationships and driving conversions.

Building an Email List

1. **Opt-In Incentives**: Entice visitors with irresistible opt-in incentives such as discounts, exclusive content, or free resources. Create compelling lead magnets that provide immediate value and incentivize subscription.

2. **Segmentation and Personalization**: Divide your email list into distinct segments based on demographics, behavior, and preferences. Tailor content and messaging to resonate with each segment, leveraging personalization tokens to enhance relevance and engagement.

Effective Email Campaigns and Automation

1. **Drip Campaigns**: Nurture leads through automated drip campaigns that deliver targeted content at key touchpoints along the customer journey. From welcome sequences to re-engagement series, drip

campaigns foster engagement and drive conversions through strategic content delivery.

2. **Behavioral Triggers**: Capitalize on user behavior triggers to deliver timely, relevant email content. Automate responses to actions such as abandoned carts, website visits, or email opens, nurturing leads and guiding them towards conversion.

2.6 Online Reputation Management

In the digital coliseum of public opinion, reputation reigns supreme. Online reputation management (ORM) is the vigilant sentinel tasked with safeguarding brand integrity amidst the tempest of user reviews, social media chatter, and digital discourse.

Monitoring and Responding to Online Reviews

1. **Vigilant Surveillance**: Monitor online review platforms, social media channels, and industry forums for mentions of your brand. Implement robust monitoring tools and processes to stay abreast of customer feedback and sentiment.

2. **Timely Responses**: Respond promptly to both positive and negative reviews, demonstrating attentiveness and commitment to customer satisfaction. Acknowledge feedback, address concerns, and offer solutions to foster goodwill and mitigate reputational damage.

Strategies for Handling Negative Feedback

1. **Transparency and Accountability**: Embrace transparency in addressing negative feedback, acknowledging mistakes, and outlining corrective actions. Demonstrate accountability and a genuine

commitment to resolving issues to rebuild trust and credibility.

2. **Turning Critics into Advocates**: Convert detractors into brand advocates through proactive engagement and resolution. Empathize with grievances, offer resolutions, and solicit feedback to transform negative experiences into opportunities for redemption and brand advocacy.

In the labyrinthine expanse of the digital landscape, building a formidable online presence is an ongoing odyssey fraught with challenges and opportunities. By embracing the principles outlined in Chapter 2, businesses can navigate the complexities of the digital realm, fortifying their virtual citadel and cultivating meaningful connections with their audience.

Chapter 3: Understanding Digital Advertising

In the vast landscape of digital advertising, navigating through its complexities can be akin to finding your way through a dense forest at night. Each pathway holds its own set of challenges, surprises, and opportunities. Let's embark on this journey, shedding light on the multifaceted world of digital advertising.

3.1 Introduction to Digital Advertising

Digital advertising serves as the modern-day marketplace, where brands vie for the attention of consumers in the vast expanse of the internet. Within this realm, two prominent contenders stand out: Paid Search and Display Advertising.

Paid Search vs. Display Advertising

Paid Search involves placing text ads within search engine results, usually at the top or bottom of the page. These ads are triggered by specific keywords, and advertisers pay a fee each time their ad is clicked, hence the term "pay-per-click" (PPC) advertising. It's like planting seeds in a well-tended garden, where the relevance of keywords determines the visibility of your ad.

Display Advertising, on the other hand, is akin to putting up billboards along the digital highways of the internet. These ads come in various formats like banners, images, or rich media, and are displayed on websites, apps, or social media platforms. Unlike paid search, display ads rely on visual appeal and targeted placement to capture audience attention.

Overview of Programmatic Advertising

Nestled within the folds of digital advertising is the phenomenon of **Programmatic Advertising**. Picture this: an intricate web of algorithms, data, and automation working tirelessly in the background to deliver ads to the right audience, at the right time, and on the right platform.

Programmatic advertising streamlines the ad buying process, enabling real-time bidding and precise targeting, akin to a finely tuned orchestra orchestrating a symphony of marketing messages.

3.2 Google Ads Fundamentals

When it comes to digital advertising, Google Ads reigns supreme, wielding immense power in the realm of online advertising.

Setting Up and Managing Google Ads Campaigns

Setting foot into the realm of Google Ads is like entering a bustling marketplace teeming with potential customers. The first step is to create a campaign, defining parameters such as ad objectives, target audience, budget, and bidding strategy. Each campaign houses ad groups, which contain specific ads tailored to distinct sets of keywords or themes. Managing these campaigns involves a delicate balance of optimization, monitoring performance metrics, and refining targeting criteria to maximize ROI.

Keyword Bidding and Budgeting

Keywords are the currency of Google Ads, and bidding on the right keywords can make or break your campaign. Advertisers engage in a bidding war, vying for the top spot in search engine results pages (SERPs). The bidding process involves setting a maximum bid for each keyword, with factors like ad quality, relevance, and historical performance influencing ad rank and placement. Budgeting is equally crucial, ensuring that ad spend aligns with campaign goals and targets.

3.3 Social Media Advertising Platforms

In the age of social media dominance, platforms like Facebook, Instagram, and LinkedIn have emerged as powerful advertising channels, offering unparalleled access to vast audiences.

Facebook Ads, Instagram Ads, LinkedIn Ads, etc.

Facebook Ads serve as the cornerstone of social media advertising, with its robust targeting options and diverse ad formats. Instagram Ads leverage the visual appeal of the platform, seamlessly integrating sponsored content into users' feeds and stories. LinkedIn Ads cater to a professional audience, offering precise targeting based on job title, industry, company size, and more. Each platform presents unique opportunities for brands to engage with their target audience in meaningful ways.

Ad Targeting Options and Best Practices

The key to success in social media advertising lies in precision targeting. Platforms like Facebook offer a treasure trove of targeting options, allowing advertisers to reach specific demographics, interests, behaviors, and even custom audiences based on website visitors or email subscribers. Best practices include A/B testing ad creatives, refining targeting criteria based on performance data, and leveraging retargeting strategies to re-engage users who have interacted with your brand.

3.4 Display Advertising Strategies

Display advertising encompasses a diverse array of formats and strategies, each designed to captivate audiences and drive engagement.

Banner Ads, Native Ads, and Retargeting

Banner Ads serve as digital billboards, commanding attention with visually striking imagery and concise messaging. **Native Ads**, seamlessly integrated into the surrounding content, blend in effortlessly with the user experience, offering a non-intrusive way to deliver branded messages. **Retargeting**, also known as remarketing, targets users who have previously interacted with your brand, serving them personalized ads across the web, reinforcing brand awareness and driving conversions.

Designing Effective Display Ad Creatives

In the realm of display advertising, creativity is king. Crafting compelling ad creatives involves striking a balance between eye-catching visuals, persuasive copywriting, and clear calls-to-action. A/B testing different ad variations allows advertisers to identify which elements resonate most with their audience, optimizing campaigns for maximum impact and ROI.

3.5 Video Advertising

Video advertising represents the pinnacle of storytelling in the digital age, offering brands a dynamic medium to convey their message and connect with audiences on a deeper level.

YouTube Advertising Basics

With over 2 billion logged-in users each month, YouTube stands as a behemoth in the realm of video advertising. TrueView ads, skippable video ads that play before, during, or after YouTube videos, offer advertisers unparalleled reach and targeting capabilities. In-stream ads appear within the video player itself, while discovery ads appear alongside search results and related videos, enticing users to engage with branded content.

Creating Compelling Video Ad Content

The key to success in video advertising lies in creating content that resonates with viewers emotionally and intellectually. Whether it's storytelling, humor, or educational content, the goal is to capture attention, evoke emotion, and inspire action. From scriptwriting to production to post-production, every aspect of the video creation process plays a crucial role in shaping the viewer's perception of the brand and driving desired outcomes.

3.6 Measuring Advertising Performance

In the realm of digital advertising, data reigns supreme, offering invaluable insights into campaign performance and ROI.

Key Advertising Metrics to Track

From clicks to conversions, a myriad of metrics offer advertisers a glimpse into the effectiveness of their campaigns. Key performance indicators (KPIs) such as click-through rate (CTR), conversion rate, cost per acquisition (CPA), and return on ad spend (ROAS) provide actionable insights into campaign performance, guiding optimization efforts and informing strategic decisions.

Analyzing and Optimizing Ad Campaigns

The journey doesn't end with launching a campaign; it's just the beginning. Continuous monitoring, analysis, and optimization are essential to ensuring ongoing success in digital advertising. A/B testing different ad creatives, refining targeting criteria, adjusting bidding strategies, and reallocating budget based on performance data are just a few tactics advertisers employ to maximize ROI and drive continuous improvement.

As we delve deeper into the intricacies of digital advertising, it becomes evident that success lies not only in mastering the tools and tactics but also in embracing creativity, adaptability, and a relentless pursuit of excellence. In this ever-evolving landscape, those who dare to innovate, experiment, and push the boundaries of possibility are the ones who will ultimately thrive

Chapter 4: Engaging with Your Audience

4.1 Building a Community Around Your Brand

In the vast landscape of digital marketing, building a community around your brand is not just a desirable strategy but often a crucial one. The importance of community engagement cannot be overstated. It goes beyond mere transactional relationships; it's about fostering a sense of belonging, loyalty, and advocacy among your audience. When your customers feel like they're part of a community, they are more likely to trust your brand, engage with your content, and become brand ambassadors themselves.

To build and nurture communities effectively, businesses must adopt various strategies. Firstly, authenticity is key. Genuine interactions and transparent communication lay the foundation for trust within your community. Secondly, consistency is vital. Regularly engaging with your audience through social media, forums, or events helps keep the community active and vibrant. Additionally, providing value through educational content, exclusive offers, or behind-the-scenes insights encourages continued participation. Lastly, listening to your community is essential. Understanding their needs, preferences, and feedback enables you to tailor your approach and strengthen the bond between your brand and its community.

4.2 Content Personalization and Customization

With the abundance of data available in the digital age, content personalization and customization have become indispensable tools for marketers. Leveraging data allows brands to deliver tailored content experiences that resonate with individual audience members, ultimately driving engagement and conversions.

Implementing dynamic content strategies involves analyzing user behavior, demographics, and preferences to create personalized experiences at scale. This can include dynamically generated website content, email campaigns tailored to specific segments, or personalized product recommendations based on past interactions.

By catering to the unique needs and interests of each customer, brands can enhance user satisfaction, increase brand loyalty, and ultimately improve their bottom line. However, it's essential to strike a balance between personalization and privacy, respecting users' data rights and preferences while still delivering value-driven experiences.

4.3 Influencer Marketing Strategies

Influencer marketing has emerged as a powerful tool for brands looking to connect with their target audience authentically. By partnering with influencers who have built trust and credibility within specific niches or demographics, brands can tap into existing communities and amplify their message effectively.

Identifying the right influencers involves thorough research to ensure alignment with your brand values, target audience, and marketing objectives. Micro-influencers, in particular, often offer higher engagement rates and greater authenticity compared to macro-influencers or celebrities.

Measuring influencer marketing ROI requires a combination of qualitative and quantitative metrics. Beyond vanity metrics such as likes and shares, brands should track key performance indicators (KPIs) like website traffic, conversions, and brand sentiment to gauge the impact of influencer partnerships accurately.

4.4 Interactive Content Strategies

In an era of short attention spans and content saturation, interactive content has emerged as a potent tool for capturing and retaining audience engagement. Quizzes, polls, contests, and interactive videos provide opportunities for active participation, fostering deeper connections between brands and consumers.

By incorporating interactive elements into their content strategy, brands can increase dwell time, encourage social sharing, and gather valuable insights about their audience preferences and behaviors. Additionally, interactive content facilitates two-way communication, allowing brands to solicit feedback, answer questions, and address concerns in real-time.

Whether it's a personality quiz, a user-generated poll, or a creative contest, interactive content sparks curiosity and encourages users to become co-creators of the brand experience. This heightened level of engagement not only drives traffic and conversions but also cultivates a sense of ownership and belonging within the community.

4.5 Customer Relationship Management (CRM)

In the digital marketing landscape, customer relationship management (CRM) plays a pivotal role in nurturing long-term customer relationships and driving business growth. CRM systems allow businesses to centralize customer data, track interactions across multiple touchpoints, and deliver personalized experiences at scale.

The importance of CRM in digital marketing extends beyond basic contact management. By leveraging customer data to segment audiences, businesses can tailor marketing campaigns, offers, and communications to specific customer segments, improving relevance and effectiveness.

Choosing and implementing the right CRM system requires careful consideration of factors such as scalability, integration capabilities, and user-friendliness. Whether opting for a cloud-based CRM solution or an on-premise deployment, businesses must ensure alignment with their organizational goals and technological infrastructure.

4.6 Harnessing the Power of User-Generated Content

User-generated content (UGC) has become a cornerstone of modern digital marketing, offering authentic, relatable, and diverse perspectives that resonate with audiences. Encouraging user reviews, testimonials, and social media mentions not only boosts brand credibility but also fosters a sense of community and belonging among customers.

Integrating user-generated content into marketing campaigns involves curating and amplifying user-created content across various channels, from social media feeds to product pages. By showcasing real-life experiences and testimonials, brands can build trust, drive engagement, and inspire action among their audience.

Moreover, UGC serves as a valuable source of market insights, providing brands with valuable feedback, product ideas, and content inspiration. By actively engaging with user-generated content and involving customers in the brand storytelling process, businesses can strengthen their relationships with their audience and foster a sense of co-ownership and collaboration.

5.1 Introduction to Digital Analytics

In the bustling world of digital marketing, data reigns supreme. The importance of data in digital marketing cannot be overstated. Every click, like, share, and purchase leaves behind a digital footprint, a treasure trove of information waiting to be mined and analyzed. Digital analytics is the key to unlocking the insights hidden within this vast sea of data, empowering marketers to make informed decisions that drive results.

Digital analytics tools play a pivotal role in this process, providing marketers with the means to collect, process, and analyze data from various digital channels. From website analytics platforms like Google Analytics to social media analytics tools like Facebook Insights and Twitter Analytics, the market is teeming with options designed to suit every need and budget. These tools offer a plethora of features, ranging from basic traffic metrics to advanced user behavior analysis, allowing marketers to gain a comprehensive understanding of their audience and their online interactions.

Importance of Data in Digital Marketing

Data is the lifeblood of digital marketing, serving as the foundation upon which successful campaigns are built. By harnessing the power of data, marketers can gain valuable insights into consumer behavior, preferences, and trends, enabling them to tailor their strategies and tactics accordingly. Whether it's optimizing website performance, refining targeting parameters, or measuring campaign effectiveness, data provides the empirical evidence needed to make informed decisions and drive tangible results.

The sheer volume and variety of data available in the digital landscape can be both a blessing and a curse. On one hand, it offers unparalleled opportunities for analysis and optimization. On the other hand, it can be overwhelming to navigate and interpret without the right tools and expertise. This is where digital analytics comes into play, offering marketers the tools and methodologies they need to make sense of the data deluge and extract actionable insights.

Overview of Analytics Tools

When it comes to digital analytics, there is no shortage of tools to choose from. Google Analytics stands out as one of the most popular and widely used platforms, offering a robust suite of features for tracking website traffic, user behavior, and conversion metrics. Its intuitive interface and extensive reporting capabilities make it a favorite among marketers of all skill levels.

In addition to Google Analytics, there are a plethora of other analytics tools available, each with its own unique features and capabilities. From social media analytics platforms like Sprout Social and Hootsuite to email marketing tools like Mailchimp and Constant Contact, the options are virtually endless. The key is to find the right combination of tools that align with your specific goals and objectives, allowing you to collect, analyze, and act on data in a meaningful way.

5.2 Website Analytics Basics

Your website is your digital storefront, the virtual gateway through which customers enter your world. Understanding how visitors interact with your website is crucial to optimizing its performance and driving desired outcomes. Website analytics provides valuable insights into visitor behavior, preferences, and actions, helping you identify areas for improvement and opportunities for growth.

Google Analytics Setup and Navigation

Setting up Google Analytics is the first step towards unlocking the full potential of your website data. Fortunately, Google provides a wealth of resources and tutorials to guide you through the process, making it accessible even to those with limited technical expertise. Once set up, navigating the Google Analytics dashboard is relatively straightforward, with intuitive menus and customizable reports that allow you to drill down into specific metrics and dimensions.

From tracking overall traffic volume and sources to monitoring user engagement and conversion rates, Google Analytics offers a comprehensive suite of features for analyzing website performance. Whether you're a small business owner looking to understand your audience better or a seasoned marketer seeking to optimize conversion funnels, Google Analytics has you covered.

Understanding Website Traffic and Behavior

Website traffic is more than just a number; it's a window into the minds of your audience. By understanding where your traffic is coming from, what pages they're visiting, and how they're navigating your site, you can gain valuable insights into their needs and preferences. Are they coming from organic search, social media, or referral links? Are they spending time on your product pages or bouncing away after a few seconds? These are the questions that website analytics can help you answer.

In addition to traffic volume and sources, website analytics also provides insights into user behavior and engagement. Metrics like bounce rate, time on page, and pages per session offer valuable clues about the effectiveness of your website content and design. Armed with this information, you can make informed decisions about optimizing your website for better user experience and conversion rates.

5.3 Social Media Analytics

Social media has become an indispensable part of the digital marketing landscape, offering unparalleled opportunities for brands to connect with their audience on a personal level. Social media analytics allows marketers to track and analyze various metrics related to their social media presence, from engagement and reach to follower demographics and content performance.

Analyzing Engagement and Reach

Engagement is the lifeblood of social media marketing, measuring the level of interaction and interaction between brands and their audience. Likes, comments, shares, and retweets are all indicators of engagement, reflecting the degree to which your content resonates with your audience. Social media analytics tools provide insights into engagement metrics, allowing you to track trends over time and identify high-performing content that drives meaningful interactions.

Reach is another critical metric in social media analytics, measuring the size and scope of your audience. How many people are seeing your posts, and how often are they being shared with others? Understanding reach allows you to gauge the effectiveness of your social media strategy and identify opportunities for expanding your audience reach.

Extracting Insights from Social Media Metrics

Social media analytics goes beyond surface-level metrics like likes and shares, delving deeper into the nuances of audience behavior and preferences. By analyzing demographic data, sentiment analysis, and content performance metrics, marketers can gain a deeper understanding of their audience and tailor their content strategy accordingly.

For example, demographic insights can help you identify key segments within your audience and develop targeted messaging that resonates with their interests and needs. Sentiment analysis allows you to gauge the overall sentiment towards your brand and products, identifying areas for improvement and potential crisis situations. Content performance metrics, such as top-performing posts and most engaging content types, provide valuable insights into what resonates with your audience and drives meaningful interactions.

5.4 Email Campaign Analytics

Email marketing remains one of the most effective channels for reaching and engaging customers, with an average ROI of $42 for every $1 spent. However, measuring the success of email campaigns goes beyond simply counting opens and clicks. Email campaign analytics allows marketers to track a wide range of metrics, from open rates and click-through rates to conversion rates and revenue generated.

Tracking Email Open Rates, Click-Through Rates, etc.

Open rate and click-through rate are two of the most commonly tracked metrics in email campaign analytics, providing insights into the effectiveness of your email content and subject lines. Open rate measures the percentage of recipients who open your email, while click-through rate measures the percentage of recipients who click on a link or call-to-action within your email. These metrics help you gauge the overall engagement and effectiveness of your email campaigns, allowing you to identify areas for improvement and optimization.

In addition to open and click-through rates, email campaign analytics also tracks conversion metrics such as conversion rate and revenue generated. Conversion rate measures the percentage of recipients who take a desired action, such as making a purchase or signing up for a newsletter, after clicking on a link within your email. By tracking conversion metrics, you can assess the bottom-line impact of your email campaigns and optimize them for maximum effectiveness.

Using Data to Optimize Email Campaigns

Data-driven optimization is the key to unlocking the full potential of your email marketing efforts. By analyzing email campaign data, marketers can identify trends, patterns, and insights that inform future campaign strategy and tactics. For example, A/B testing allows you to experiment with different email content, subject lines, and calls-to-action to see which perform best with your audience.

Segmentation is another powerful strategy for optimizing email campaigns, allowing you to target specific segments of your audience with personalized messaging and offers. By segmenting your email list based on factors such as demographics, purchase history, and engagement level, you can deliver more relevant and timely content that resonates with your audience and drives results.

5.5 Advertising Analytics

Advertising is a cornerstone of digital marketing, allowing brands to reach and engage with their target audience across a wide range of channels and platforms. Advertising analytics provides insights into the performance of advertising campaigns, helping marketers measure ROI, track key metrics, and optimize their advertising spend for maximum impact.

Measuring ROI of Advertising Campaigns

ROI is the ultimate measure of advertising effectiveness, quantifying the return on investment generated by your advertising efforts. By comparing the cost of your advertising campaign to the revenue generated as a result, you can calculate ROI and assess the overall profitability of your advertising efforts. Advertising analytics tools provide the data and insights needed to track ROI across various advertising channels and platforms, allowing you to identify high-performing campaigns and allocate your budget accordingly.

Attribution Models and Conversion Tracking

Attribution modeling is a critical component of advertising analytics, helping marketers understand the role that each advertising touchpoint plays in the customer journey. By assigning credit to each touchpoint based on its influence on the final conversion, attribution models provide insights into the effectiveness of different advertising channels and tactics. From first-click attribution to multi-touch attribution models, there are various approaches to attribution modeling, each offering unique insights into the customer journey and the impact of advertising on conversion rates.

Conversion tracking is another essential aspect of advertising analytics, allowing marketers to track and measure the actions taken by users after interacting with an ad. Whether it's making a purchase, signing up for a newsletter, or downloading a whitepaper, conversion tracking provides valuable insights into the effectiveness of your advertising campaigns and helps you optimize them for maximum impact.

5.6 Data-Driven Decision Making

In the fast-paced world of digital marketing, data-driven decision-making is essential for staying ahead of the curve and driving meaningful results. By leveraging data to inform marketing strategies and tactics, marketers can gain a competitive edge and achieve their business objectives more effectively.

Using Data to Inform Marketing Strategies

Data serves as a compass guiding marketers towards their goals, providing valuable insights and intelligence that inform strategic decision-making. Whether it's identifying new market opportunities, refining target audience segments, or optimizing campaign performance, data provides the empirical evidence needed to make informed decisions and drive tangible results. From market research and competitive analysis to customer segmentation and persona development, data plays a central role in every aspect of the marketing process.

A/B Testing and Experimentation in Digital Marketing

A/B testing is a cornerstone of data-driven decision-making, allowing marketers to experiment with different variations of a marketing asset to see which performs best with their audience. Whether it's testing different ad creatives, email subject lines, or website designs, A/B testing provides valuable insights into what resonates with your audience and drives desired outcomes. By systematically testing and iterating on different variables, marketers can optimize their marketing efforts for maximum impact and continuously improve performance over time.

In conclusion, digital analytics is the cornerstone of modern marketing, providing marketers with the tools and insights they need to make informed decisions and drive meaningful results. From website analytics and social media analytics to email campaign analytics and advertising analytics, the digital landscape offers a wealth of opportunities for data-driven optimization and experimentation. By embracing digital analytics and harnessing the power of data, marketers can unlock new levels of success and achieve their business objectives more effectively than ever before.

6.1 Mobile Marketing Strategies

In today's digital landscape, mobile marketing has become a cornerstone of any successful marketing strategy. The ubiquity of smartphones and tablets has revolutionized the way businesses interact with their audiences. Mobile optimization is not just a luxury but a necessity for brands looking to thrive in the digital space. The importance of mobile optimization cannot be overstated. With a significant portion of internet traffic originating from mobile devices, failing to optimize for mobile can result in missed opportunities, decreased engagement, and ultimately, loss of revenue.

Importance of Mobile Optimization

1. **User Experience (UX)**: Mobile optimization directly impacts user experience. Websites that are not optimized for mobile devices often suffer from slow loading times, distorted

layouts, and difficult navigation. This leads to frustration among users, resulting in high bounce rates and lower conversions.

2. **Search Engine Ranking**: Search engines like Google prioritize mobile-friendly websites in their rankings. Mobile optimization is a crucial factor in search engine optimization (SEO). Websites that are not optimized for mobile are likely to rank lower in search engine results pages (SERPs), thereby reducing visibility and organic traffic.

3. **Accessibility**: Mobile optimization enhances accessibility, making it easier for users to access content on the go. With the increasing reliance on mobile devices for internet access, ensuring that your website is accessible across various

screen sizes and devices is imperative for reaching a wider audience.

Mobile-First Website Design Principles

1. **Responsive Design**: Adopting a responsive design approach ensures that your website adapts seamlessly to different screen sizes and resolutions. Responsive design allows for fluid scaling of elements, optimizing the user experience across devices.

2. **Fast Loading Times**: Mobile users have limited patience for slow-loading websites. Implementing strategies to optimize loading times, such as minimizing HTTP requests, optimizing images, and leveraging browser caching, is essential for providing a smooth browsing experience.

3. **Thumb-Friendly Navigation**: Designing with mobile users in mind involves placing navigation menus and interactive elements within easy reach of the user's thumb. This ergonomic approach enhances usability and reduces friction in the browsing experience.

4. **Optimized Content Layout**: Content should be structured and formatted for readability on small screens. Prioritize concise, scannable content and avoid cluttering the screen with unnecessary elements. Clear, concise calls-to-action are essential for guiding users through the conversion process.

6.2 Location-Based Marketing

Location-based marketing leverages geographical data to target and engage audiences in specific geographic locations. By harnessing the power of location intelligence, businesses can deliver highly relevant and personalized experiences to consumers based on their physical proximity.

Geotargeting and Geofencing

1. **Geotargeting**: Geotargeting allows marketers to deliver tailored content or promotions to users based on their geographic location. This could involve displaying location-specific advertisements, offering localized deals, or providing directions to nearby physical stores.

2. **Geofencing**: Geofencing involves setting up virtual perimeters around physical locations. When a user enters or exits a geofenced area, they can receive targeted notifications or promotions via mobile apps. Geofencing is particularly effective for driving foot traffic to brick-and-mortar

stores and enhancing the overall customer experience.

Strategies for Reaching Local Audiences

1. **Local SEO**: Optimizing your online presence for local search is crucial for reaching local audiences. This includes optimizing Google My Business listings, incorporating location-specific keywords into website content, and earning citations from local directories.

2. **Local Content Marketing**: Creating locally relevant content can help attract and engage local audiences. This could include blog posts, videos, or social media content that highlights local events, trends, or community initiatives.

3. **Community Engagement**: Actively engaging with the local community through sponsorships, events, or

partnerships can foster brand loyalty and strengthen connections with local audiences. Participating in local events or sponsoring local charities can help raise brand awareness and build trust within the community.

6.3 Mobile Advertising Platforms

Mobile advertising platforms offer businesses a variety of channels and formats to reach their target audience effectively on mobile devices. From display ads to in-app advertising, these platforms provide opportunities for brands to engage users where they spend a significant amount of their digital time.

Mobile Display Ads, In-App Advertising, etc.

1. **Mobile Display Ads**: Mobile display ads appear on websites and apps viewed on mobile devices. These ads can take the form of banners, interstitials, or native ads and are often served

programmatically through ad networks or exchanges.

2. **In-App Advertising**: In-app advertising involves displaying ads within mobile applications. These ads can be static banners, video ads, or interactive rich media ads. In-app advertising allows advertisers to reach users while they are actively engaged with content, maximizing the impact of their campaigns.

Ad Formats and Best Practices for Mobile

1. **Responsive Ad Design**: Ad creatives should be optimized for mobile viewing, with clear imagery, concise copy, and prominent calls-to-action. Responsive ad design ensures that ads display correctly across various screen sizes and orientations.

2. **Native Advertising**: Native ads seamlessly blend into the surrounding content, providing a non-disruptive user experience. By aligning with the look and feel of the platform, native ads can achieve higher engagement rates and better performance compared to traditional display ads.

3. **Video Advertising**: With the popularity of video content on mobile devices, video advertising presents a powerful opportunity for brands to capture audience attention. Short, captivating videos optimized for mobile viewing can effectively convey brand messages and drive conversions.

6.4 Optimizing for Voice Search

The proliferation of voice-activated devices and virtual assistants has transformed the way users search for information and interact with technology. Optimizing content for voice search is essential for ensuring visibility and relevance in an increasingly voice-centric world.

Understanding the Rise of Voice Assistants

1. **Growing Adoption**: Voice assistants such as Amazon Alexa, Google Assistant, and Apple Siri have seen rapid adoption in recent years, becoming integral parts of users' daily lives. The convenience and hands-free nature of voice search have contributed to its popularity among consumers.

2. **Natural Language Processing**: Voice search relies on natural language processing (NLP) algorithms to understand user queries and provide relevant responses. Optimizing content for natural language and conversational queries is key to appearing in voice search results.

Optimizing Content for Voice Search Queries

1. **Long-Tail Keywords**: Voice search queries tend to be more conversational and longer than traditional text-based searches. Incorporating long-tail keywords and phrases that mirror natural speech patterns can improve the likelihood of appearing in voice search results.

2. **FAQ Optimization**: Anticipating and addressing common questions and queries related to your business or industry can help optimize content for voice search. Creating FAQ pages or structured content that directly answers user queries can increase visibility in voice search results.

3. **Local Optimization**: Optimizing for local search is particularly important for voice searches with local intent. This involves

optimizing business listings, incorporating location-specific keywords, and ensuring consistency across online directories and platforms.

6.5 Mobile App Marketing

As mobile app usage continues to soar, effective app marketing strategies are essential for driving app discovery, user acquisition, and engagement. App Store Optimization (ASO) and targeted user acquisition campaigns play key roles in maximizing app visibility and success.

App Store Optimization (ASO)

1. **Keyword Optimization**: Optimizing app metadata, including app title, description, and keywords, is crucial for improving app visibility in app store search results. Conducting keyword research and monitoring keyword performance can help refine ASO strategies over time.

2. **App Ratings and Reviews**: Positive app ratings and reviews are critical for building trust and credibility among potential users. Encouraging satisfied users to leave reviews and promptly addressing negative feedback can help maintain a positive app reputation.

User Acquisition and Retention Strategies for Apps

1. **Targeted Advertising**: Leveraging targeted advertising campaigns across various channels, including social media, search, and display networks, can effectively reach potential app users. By targeting specific demographics, interests, and behaviors, advertisers can maximize campaign ROI and drive app installs.

2. **Engagement Campaigns**: Implementing engagement campaigns, such as push notifications, in-app messaging, and

personalized content recommendations, can help retain and re-engage app users. Providing value-added features, exclusive content, or rewards can incentivize continued app usage and loyalty.

6.6 Measuring Mobile and Local Marketing Effectiveness

Measuring the effectiveness of mobile and local marketing initiatives is essential for optimizing campaign performance, allocating resources effectively, and maximizing return on investment (ROI). Mobile analytics tools and metrics provide valuable insights into user behavior, campaign effectiveness, and overall business impact.

Mobile Analytics Tools and Metrics

1. **App Analytics**: Mobile app analytics platforms, such as Google Analytics for Firebase and Appsflyer, provide comprehensive insights into app usage, user engagement, retention, and

monetization. Key metrics include app installs, active users, session duration, and in-app purchases.

2. **Website Analytics**: Web analytics tools, such as Google Analytics, offer valuable insights into mobile website performance, traffic sources, user behavior, and conversion metrics. Tracking metrics such as mobile traffic, bounce rate, and conversion rate can help optimize mobile website user experience and conversion funnel.

Evaluating Local Campaign Performance and ROI

1. **Geolocation Data**: Utilizing geolocation data can help evaluate the effectiveness of local marketing campaigns by tracking foot traffic, store visits, and conversion rates at specific locations. Geo-targeted advertising platforms and location-based

analytics tools offer insights into campaign reach and engagement at the local level.

2. **ROI Analysis**: Calculating return on investment (ROI) for mobile and local marketing campaigns involves comparing campaign costs to measurable outcomes, such as app installs, website conversions, or store visits. By attributing conversions to specific marketing channels or campaigns, businesses can assess the effectiveness of their marketing efforts and make data-driven decisions for future initiatives.

In conclusion, optimizing for mobile and local audiences requires a multifaceted approach that encompasses mobile marketing strategies, location-based marketing tactics, and robust measurement and analytics frameworks. By prioritizing mobile optimization, leveraging location intelligence, and adopting data-driven marketing practices, businesses can effectively engage with their target audiences in an increasingly mobile-centric and geographically diverse digital landscape.

Chapter 7: E-commerce and Online Sales Strategies

E-commerce has transformed the way businesses operate, revolutionizing the shopping experience for consumers worldwide. In this chapter, we delve into various aspects of e-commerce, from its introduction and different business models to strategies for creating seamless shopping experiences, optimizing for search engines, recovering from cart abandonment, implementing personalization, and ensuring efficient fulfillment and customer service.

7.1 Introduction to E-commerce

E-commerce Platforms and Marketplaces:

E-commerce platforms and marketplaces serve as the digital infrastructure for online businesses to showcase and sell their products or services. These platforms range from self-hosted solutions like Shopify and WooCommerce to third-party marketplaces such as Amazon and eBay. Each platform offers unique features and caters to different business needs, whether it's ease of use, scalability, or access to a large customer base.

Types of E-commerce Business Models:

E-commerce encompasses various business models, each with its own set of advantages and challenges. Some common types include Business-to-Consumer (B2C), where businesses sell directly to consumers; Business-to-Business (B2B), involving transactions between businesses; Consumer-to-Consumer (C2C), where individuals sell to other individuals through platforms like eBay; and Dropshipping, where retailers fulfill orders through third-party suppliers without holding inventory. Each model requires tailored strategies for marketing, logistics, and customer engagement.

7.2 Creating a Seamless Online Shopping Experience

User-Friendly Navigation and Checkout Process:

A seamless online shopping experience begins with intuitive website navigation and a streamlined checkout process. Users should be able to easily find products, browse categories, and add items to their carts without encountering any obstacles. Implementing clear navigation menus, search functionality, and progress indicators during checkout can significantly enhance user satisfaction and reduce cart abandonment rates.

Implementing Secure Payment Gateways:

Security is paramount in e-commerce, especially when handling sensitive customer information during payment transactions. Implementing secure payment gateways that encrypt data and comply with industry standards such as PCI DSS (Payment Card Industry Data Security Standard) is essential for building trust with customers. Additionally, offering multiple payment options, including credit cards, digital wallets, and alternative payment methods, caters to diverse customer preferences and increases conversion rates.

7.3 E-commerce SEO and SEM

Optimizing Product Pages for Search:

Search engine optimization (SEO) plays a crucial role in driving organic traffic to e-commerce websites. Optimizing product pages with relevant keywords, compelling product descriptions, and high-quality images can improve search engine rankings and visibility. Additionally, leveraging structured data markup, optimizing meta tags, and improving page load speed contribute to better SEO performance and increased organic search traffic.

Running Paid Search Campaigns for E-commerce:

In addition to SEO, e-commerce businesses can boost their online visibility through paid search advertising, commonly referred to as search engine marketing (SEM) or pay-per-click (PPC) advertising. Platforms like Google Ads and Bing Ads allow businesses to target specific keywords, demographics, and geographic locations to reach their target audience effectively. By strategically allocating advertising budgets and monitoring campaign performance, e-commerce retailers can maximize ROI and drive sales.

7.4 Cart Abandonment Recovery Strategies

Understanding Cart Abandonment Causes:

Cart abandonment occurs when shoppers add items to their carts but leave the website without completing the purchase. Understanding the reasons behind cart abandonment, such as unexpected shipping costs, complex checkout processes, or lack of trust, is crucial for implementing effective recovery strategies. Conducting user research, analyzing website analytics, and soliciting feedback can provide insights into addressing common pain points and improving conversion rates.

Implementing Email Remarketing and Exit-Intent Popups:

Email remarketing and exit-intent popups are effective tools for re-engaging with customers who abandon their carts. Sending personalized email reminders with incentives such as discounts or free shipping can prompt customers to return and complete their purchases. Exit-intent popups, triggered when a user attempts to leave the website, can offer discounts or capture email addresses for future remarketing efforts. By strategically timing these interventions, e-commerce retailers can recover lost sales and nurture customer relationships.

7.5 Personalization in E-commerce

Product Recommendations and Dynamic Pricing:

Personalization enhances the shopping experience by presenting relevant products and pricing tailored to each customer's preferences and behavior. Utilizing algorithms and machine learning, e-commerce platforms can analyze customer data such as browsing history, purchase patterns, and demographics to deliver personalized product recommendations and dynamic pricing. By anticipating customer needs and preferences, businesses can increase sales and customer loyalty while reducing decision fatigue.

Using Customer Data to Customize Shopping Experience:

Collecting and analyzing customer data is essential for delivering personalized shopping experiences in e-commerce. By leveraging data analytics tools and customer relationship management (CRM) systems, businesses can gain insights into individual customer preferences, shopping behaviors, and lifecycle stages. This data enables targeted marketing campaigns, personalized communication, and customized product offerings that resonate with customers on a personal level, ultimately driving engagement and sales.

7.6 Fulfillment and Customer Service in E-commerce

Order Fulfillment Strategies:

Efficient order fulfillment is critical for delivering a positive post-purchase experience and building customer loyalty. E-commerce businesses must optimize their fulfillment processes, from inventory management and order processing to shipping and delivery. Implementing inventory management software, integrating with third-party logistics providers, and offering flexible shipping options such as same-day or next-day delivery can streamline operations and exceed customer expectations.

Providing Excellent Customer Support in Online Retail:

Customer support is a cornerstone of successful e-commerce operations, serving as a point of contact for inquiries, assistance, and issue resolution. Offering multiple channels of communication, including live chat, email, and phone support, enables customers to reach out conveniently and receive timely assistance. Investing in training for support staff, implementing self-service resources such as FAQs and knowledge bases, and proactively addressing customer concerns contribute to a positive customer service experience and foster long-term relationships.

In conclusion, e-commerce presents vast opportunities for businesses to reach global audiences, drive sales, and deliver exceptional shopping experiences. By leveraging e-commerce platforms, implementing effective strategies for

SEO, SEM, and cart abandonment recovery, personalizing the shopping journey, and prioritizing fulfillment and customer service, businesses can thrive in the digital marketplace and build sustainable success.

Chapter 8: Emerging Trends in Digital Marketing

Digital marketing is an ever-evolving landscape, continually shaped by technological advancements and changing consumer behaviors. In this chapter, we delve into the emerging trends that are reshaping the digital marketing landscape, from the integration of artificial intelligence to the rise of immersive experiences and the growing importance of privacy and data protection.

8.1 Artificial Intelligence (AI) in Marketing

Artificial Intelligence (AI) has revolutionized the way marketers engage with their audience, offering unprecedented insights and capabilities. AI-powered marketing automation is at the forefront of this revolution, allowing marketers to streamline repetitive tasks, personalize content at scale, and optimize campaigns in real-time. Through machine learning algorithms, AI analyzes vast amounts of data to identify patterns and predict future outcomes, enabling more effective targeting and conversion optimization.

AI-Powered Marketing Automation

One of the most significant benefits of AI-powered marketing automation is its ability to enhance efficiency and productivity. By automating repetitive tasks such as email marketing, social media posting, and ad optimization, marketers can free up valuable time to focus on strategic initiatives and creative endeavors. Moreover, AI enables hyper-personalization by analyzing customer data to deliver tailored content and recommendations, resulting in higher engagement and conversion rates.

Predictive Analytics and Customer Segmentation

Predictive analytics, powered by AI, enables marketers to anticipate customer behavior and preferences based on historical data and real-time interactions. By leveraging predictive models, marketers can segment their audience more effectively and deliver targeted messaging that resonates with specific segments. This level of granularity allows for more precise targeting and personalized experiences, ultimately driving higher ROI and customer satisfaction.

8.2 Voice Search and Smart Speakers

The proliferation of voice-activated devices and smart speakers has fundamentally changed the way consumers search for information and interact with brands. As voice search continues to gain traction, marketers must adapt their strategies to optimize for this emerging channel and capitalize on the opportunities it presents.

Optimizing for Voice Search Queries

Optimizing content for voice search requires a different approach than traditional SEO tactics. Since voice queries tend to be more conversational and long-tail, marketers need to focus on natural language and contextually relevant content. This includes incorporating question-based keywords, providing concise answers to common queries, and optimizing for local search intent to capture "near me" queries.

Marketing Opportunities with Smart Speakers

Smart speakers offer a unique platform for brands to engage with consumers in their homes through voice-activated assistants like Amazon Alexa and Google Assistant. Marketers can leverage smart speakers to deliver personalized content, facilitate voice-based transactions, and even create interactive experiences such as voice-activated games and quizzes. By integrating with popular voice platforms, brands can extend their reach and foster deeper connections with their audience.

8.3 Augmented Reality (AR) and Virtual Reality (VR) Marketing

Augmented Reality (AR) and Virtual Reality (VR) have transformed the way brands engage with consumers, offering immersive experiences that blur the line between the digital and physical worlds. From interactive product demonstrations to virtual storefronts, AR and VR are opening up new possibilities for marketers to captivate audiences and drive brand engagement.

Enhancing Customer Experience with AR/VR

AR and VR technologies enable brands to create immersive experiences that bring their products and services to life in ways previously unimaginable. Whether it's trying on virtual clothing, exploring virtual showrooms, or visualizing home decor in AR, these experiences enable consumers to engage with brands on a deeper level and make more informed purchasing decisions. By leveraging AR and VR, marketers can enhance the customer experience and differentiate their brand in a crowded marketplace.

AR/VR Advertising Opportunities

In addition to enhancing the customer experience, AR and VR offer unique advertising opportunities for brands looking to stand out in a cluttered digital landscape. Whether through sponsored AR filters on social media platforms like Snapchat and Instagram or immersive VR ad experiences, brands can capture consumers' attention in highly engaging and memorable ways. These immersive ad formats enable brands to tell compelling stories, showcase products in context, and drive higher levels of brand recall and affinity.

8.4 Chatbots and Conversational Marketing

Chatbots have become an integral part of the digital marketing toolkit, enabling brands to deliver personalized, real-time support and streamline customer interactions. By leveraging artificial intelligence and natural language processing, chatbots can engage customers in meaningful conversations, drive lead generation, and enhance the overall customer experience.

Implementing Chatbots for Customer Support

One of the primary applications of chatbots in marketing is customer support automation. By deploying chatbots on websites, social media platforms, and messaging apps, brands can provide instant assistance to customers, answer frequently asked questions, and resolve common issues without human intervention. This not only improves efficiency and scalability but also enables brands to deliver round-the-clock support and enhance customer satisfaction.

Using Chatbots for Lead Generation and Sales

In addition to customer support, chatbots are also effective tools for lead generation and sales. By engaging visitors in personalized conversations, qualifying leads, and guiding them through the sales funnel, chatbots can significantly improve conversion rates and revenue generation. Furthermore, chatbots can integrate seamlessly with e-commerce platforms to facilitate transactions, recommend products, and provide order status updates, thereby enhancing the overall shopping experience.

8.5 Video Marketing Trends

Video has become the dominant form of content consumption online, with platforms like YouTube, TikTok, and Instagram driving unprecedented levels of engagement. Marketers are increasingly leveraging video content to capture consumers' attention, tell compelling stories, and drive action across the customer journey.

Short-Form Video Content (e.g., TikTok)

Short-form video content has exploded in popularity, thanks to platforms like TikTok and Instagram Reels. These bite-sized videos offer a quick and entertaining way for brands to connect with their audience and showcase their personality. Whether it's behind-the-scenes footage, user-generated content, or viral challenges, short-form videos enable brands to cut through the noise and resonate with consumers in a memorable way.

Live Streaming and Interactive Video Experiences

Live streaming has emerged as a powerful tool for brands to engage with their audience in real-time and foster authentic connections. Whether it's hosting Q&A sessions, product launches, or live events, live streaming enables brands to humanize their brand, solicit immediate feedback, and drive engagement through interactive features like chat and polls. By harnessing the power of live video, marketers can create immersive experiences that captivate audiences and drive meaningful action.

8.6 Privacy and Data Protection in Digital Marketing

As consumers become increasingly concerned about their privacy and data security, brands must prioritize transparency and accountability in their digital marketing practices. Building trust through transparent data practices and compliance with data protection regulations is essential for maintaining consumer trust and loyalty.

Compliance with Data Protection Regulations

With the implementation of regulations like GDPR and CCPA, brands are required to adhere to strict guidelines regarding the collection, use, and storage of consumer data. This includes obtaining explicit consent for data processing, providing clear privacy policies, and honoring individuals' rights regarding their personal information. Failure to comply with these regulations can result in hefty fines and reputational damage, highlighting the importance of robust data protection measures.

Building Trust through Transparent Data Practices

Transparency is key to building trust with consumers in the digital age. Brands must be transparent about how they collect, use, and protect consumer data, providing clear explanations and options for individuals to control their privacy settings. By prioritizing transparency and accountability, brands can foster trust and confidence among their audience, ultimately driving long-term loyalty and brand advocacy.

In conclusion, the digital marketing landscape is constantly evolving, driven by technological innovations and shifting consumer preferences. By embracing emerging trends such as artificial intelligence, voice search, AR/VR, chatbots, video marketing, and prioritizing privacy and data protection, brands can stay ahead of the curve and create meaningful connections with their audience in an increasingly digital world.

Chapter 9: Crafting Your Digital Marketing Strategy

In the fast-paced and ever-evolving landscape of digital marketing, crafting an effective strategy is paramount for businesses aiming to thrive in the online realm. This chapter delves into the intricacies of devising a comprehensive digital marketing strategy, covering essential aspects from assessing the current marketing situation to continuous learning and adaptation.

9.1 Assessing Your Current Marketing Situation

Before embarking on any strategic endeavors, it's imperative to conduct a thorough examination of your current marketing landscape through a process known as a marketing audit. This involves scrutinizing all facets of your existing marketing efforts to gain insights into what's working, what's not, and where improvements can be made. A marketing audit typically entails:

Conducting a Marketing Audit

A marketing audit encompasses an in-depth analysis of various components, including branding, messaging, channels, and performance metrics. It involves scrutinizing past campaigns, customer feedback, competitor activities, and market trends. By dissecting each element of your marketing initiatives, you can unearth valuable insights into areas of strength and weakness, enabling informed decision-making for future strategies.

Identifying Strengths, Weaknesses, Opportunities, and Threats (SWOT)

Utilizing the SWOT analysis framework is instrumental in distilling the findings of the marketing audit into actionable insights. This involves identifying internal strengths and weaknesses, such as unique brand propositions and operational inefficiencies, as well as external opportunities and threats, such as emerging market trends and competitive pressures. The SWOT analysis serves as a strategic compass, guiding the formulation of a robust digital marketing strategy grounded in a clear understanding of the business's position within its industry.

9.2 Defining Your Target Audience and Value Proposition

Central to any effective marketing strategy is a deep understanding of the target audience and a compelling value proposition that resonates with their needs and preferences.

Creating Detailed Buyer Personas

Developing comprehensive buyer personas is a fundamental step in defining your target audience. These personas represent semi-fictional representations of your ideal customers, encompassing demographic information, behaviors, pain points, and goals. By delving into the psyche of your target audience segments, you can tailor your marketing efforts to address their specific needs and aspirations, fostering stronger connections and driving engagement.

Articulating Your Unique Selling Proposition (USP)

A compelling Unique Selling Proposition (USP) forms the cornerstone of your value proposition, setting your brand apart from competitors in the crowded digital marketplace. Your USP encapsulates the unique benefits and value that your products or services offer to customers, compelling them to choose your brand over alternatives. Whether it's superior quality, unmatched convenience, or innovative features, a well-defined USP serves as a powerful differentiator, attracting and retaining customers amidst fierce competition.

9.3 Developing a Comprehensive Marketing Plan

With a clear understanding of the market landscape, target audience, and value proposition, the next step is to translate these insights into a comprehensive marketing plan that outlines clear objectives, strategies, and resource allocations.

Setting Clear Objectives and Strategies

Effective marketing plans start with clearly defined objectives that align with overarching business goals. Whether it's increasing brand awareness, driving website traffic, or boosting sales conversions, each objective should be SMART (Specific, Measurable, Achievable, Relevant, Time-bound). Accompanying these objectives are well-crafted strategies that delineate the approach to achieving them, encompassing tactics, channels, and timelines.

Allocating Budget and Resources Effectively

Allocating budget and resources judiciously is critical for maximizing the impact of your marketing efforts. This involves balancing investments across various channels and tactics based on their efficacy in reaching and engaging the target audience. Whether it's allocating funds for social media advertising, content creation, or SEO optimization, strategic resource allocation ensures optimal utilization of available resources for maximum return on investment (ROI).

9.4 Implementation and Execution

Execution is where strategy meets action, and effective implementation is essential for bringing your marketing plan to fruition.

Setting Up Tracking and Analytics Systems

Implementing robust tracking and analytics systems is vital for monitoring the performance of your marketing initiatives and deriving actionable insights. By leveraging tools such as Google Analytics, social media analytics platforms, and CRM systems, you can track key metrics, measure campaign effectiveness, and gain deeper visibility into customer behavior. This data-driven approach empowers informed decision-making and enables iterative optimization of marketing strategies.

Launching and Managing Marketing Campaigns

Launching and managing marketing campaigns require meticulous planning, coordination, and execution across various channels and touchpoints. Whether it's email marketing, PPC advertising, or influencer partnerships, each campaign must be tailored to resonate with the target audience and achieve predefined objectives. Effective campaign management involves continuous monitoring, optimization, and iteration based on real-time performance data and customer feedback.

9.5 Monitoring and Measuring Performance

In the dynamic realm of digital marketing, monitoring and measuring performance are indispensable for evaluating the effectiveness of your strategies and making data-driven adjustments.

Regularly Reviewing Key Metrics and KPIs

Key Performance Indicators (KPIs) serve as quantifiable benchmarks for assessing the success of your marketing efforts. These metrics encompass a range of variables, including website traffic, conversion rates, customer acquisition cost, and return on investment. Regularly reviewing KPIs provides valuable insights into the performance of individual campaigns and overall marketing initiatives, enabling timely course corrections and optimization strategies.

Making Data-Driven Adjustments to Strategy

Data-driven decision-making lies at the heart of effective marketing strategy refinement. By analyzing performance data, identifying trends, and discerning patterns, marketers can uncover areas for improvement and refine their strategies accordingly. Whether it's tweaking messaging, adjusting targeting parameters, or reallocating resources, data-driven adjustments ensure that marketing efforts remain agile and responsive to evolving market dynamics.

9.6 Continuous Learning and Adaptation

In the rapidly evolving landscape of digital marketing, staying abreast of industry trends and best practices is essential for staying ahead of the curve and maintaining a competitive edge.

Staying Updated on Industry Trends and Best Practices

Continuous learning and professional development are imperative for marketers seeking to excel in their field. This involves staying updated on emerging technologies, consumer behavior shifts, and evolving market dynamics through industry publications, conferences, and online courses. By embracing a culture of lifelong learning, marketers can adapt their strategies to capitalize on new opportunities and navigate challenges effectively.

Iterating and Improving Your Digital Marketing Strategy Over Time

The digital marketing landscape is characterized by constant change and evolution, necessitating a proactive approach to strategy iteration and improvement. By soliciting feedback, analyzing performance data, and embracing a mindset of experimentation, marketers can iteratively refine their strategies to optimize results and drive sustainable growth. This iterative approach enables continuous improvement and ensures that digital marketing efforts remain agile and adaptive in the face of evolving market dynamics.

In conclusion to this crafting a successful digital marketing strategy requires a blend of strategic foresight, data-driven decision-making, and a commitment to continuous improvement. By assessing the current marketing situation, defining target audiences and value propositions, developing comprehensive marketing plans, and embracing a culture of learning and adaptation, businesses can navigate the complexities of the digital landscape with confidence and achieve their marketing objectives effectively.

Conclusion

As we conclude our exploration of digital marketing for beginners in 2024, it's evident that the landscape of online promotion continues to evolve at a rapid pace. This journey through the fundamentals of digital marketing has illuminated key strategies, tools, and trends essential for newcomers embarking on their digital marketing endeavors.

First and foremost, understanding the importance of an integrated approach is paramount. Digital marketing is not a one-size-fits-all solution; rather, it's a dynamic ecosystem comprising various channels and techniques that complement each other. From search engine optimization (SEO) and content marketing to social media advertising and email campaigns, each component plays a crucial role in achieving marketing objectives.

Furthermore, the emphasis on data-driven decision-making cannot be overstated. In the digital realm, insights derived from analytics serve as the compass guiding marketing efforts. By harnessing the power of data analytics, beginners can gain invaluable insights into consumer behavior, preferences, and trends, enabling them to refine their strategies for optimal results.

Additionally, staying abreast of emerging technologies and trends is essential for remaining competitive in the ever-evolving digital landscape. As artificial intelligence, augmented reality, and voice search continue to reshape the marketing landscape, embracing innovation and experimentation becomes imperative for beginners seeking to stay ahead of the curve.

Moreover, fostering meaningful connections with audiences is the cornerstone of successful digital marketing. In an era characterized by information overload, authenticity, transparency, and personalization are more critical than ever. By creating compelling, relevant content and engaging with customers in meaningful ways, beginners can forge lasting relationships that foster loyalty and advocacy.

Lastly, it's essential to recognize that digital marketing is not merely about promoting products or services; it's about creating value for customers. By prioritizing the needs and interests of their target audience, beginners can cultivate trust, credibility, and loyalty, laying the foundation for long-term success.

In conclusion, while the world of digital marketing may seem daunting for beginners, it also presents boundless opportunities for growth and innovation. By embracing a strategic, data-driven approach, staying attuned to industry developments, and prioritizing customer-centricity, beginners can navigate the digital landscape with confidence and achieve their marketing objectives in 2024 and beyond.

www.ingramcontent.com/pod-product-compliance
Lightning Source LLC
Chambersburg PA
CBHW070147230526
45471CB00002B/557